Isabel McNeill Carley Orff Essentials Collection

Recorder Improvisation and Technique

BOOK TWO

Intermediate for Alto and Soprano Recorder

Classroom or Lesson Setting

Isabel McNeill Carley

Third Edition
Teacher and Student

Copyright © 2011-2023
Fourth Printing
Brasstown Press

B P

Brasstown Press
Charlottesville, VA
USA
brasstownpress.com

Printed in USA
ISBN 978-0-9836545-1-3

Reviews of this Edition

Plenty of lovely ideas for student improvisation, and the emphasis on doing first, then, applying literacy is still evident. Students are encouraged to move back and forth between soprano and alto fingerings, at their own pace...[and] are also challenged to build a repertoire of songs, in both fingerings, that they can play by memory. Integration of two or more other Orff media is included in every lesson.

~ **Kim Kendrick** in *Ostinato*

Builds directly on skills introduced in Book One, also introducing the alto recorder and F fingerings. On both soprano and alto recorder, 13 lessons review pentatonic keys, then explore the diatonic modes, and finally briefly introduce improvisation over chord changes....[P]rovides a wealth of material in a structured pedagogy for developing recorder technique.

~ **Leslie Timmons** in *American Recorder*

o

Comments on previous editions of Recorder Improvisation and Technique

Your recorder books are excellent ... completely in the spirit of the Schulwerk.

~ **Gunild Keetman**, co-creator, with Carl Orff, of the Orff Schulwerk

The tunes are lovely, and even the patterns are satisfying.

~ **Miriam Samuelson**, founding member of the American Orff-Schulwerk Association

Isabel Carley has given us a guide to musicianship. The recorder is only the means.

~ **Elizabeth Nichols**, founding member of the American Orff-Schulwerk Association

---

Acknowledgments

Edited and produced by Brasstown Press with production assistance from Ayla Palermo.
Cover and symbols by Browning Porter Design.
Printed in USA.

Note on the third edition

This newly designed and reset edition of **Recorder Improvisation and Technique Book Two** (**RIT Two**) retains the contents of the second edition, with the addition of expanded reference and resource materials.

CONTENTS

Major Scales & their Related Modes

	Major • *Do*	Aeolian • *La*	Dorian • *Re*	Phrygian • *Mi*	Mixolydian • *So*
C	CDEFGABC	ABCDEFGA	DEFGABCD	EFGABCDE	GABCDEFG
G	GABCDEF♯G	EF♯GABCDE	ABCDEF♯GA	BCDEF♯GAB	DEF♯GABCD
F	FGAB♭CDEF	DEFGAB♭CD	GAB♭CDEFG	AB♭CDEFGA	CDEFGAB♭C
D	DEF♯GABC♯D	BC♯DEF♯GAB	EF♯GABC♯DE	F♯GABC♯DEF♯	ABC♯DEFGA
B♭	B♭CDEFGAB♭	GAB♭CDE♭FG	CDE♭FGAB♭C	DE♭FGAB♭CD	FGAB♭CDE♭F

Hand Signs

Do' =

[Eye level]

Ti =

La =

So =

Fa =

Mi =

Re =

Do =

[Waist height]

Instruments & Abbreviations

Recorders

Nino	Sopranino Recorder
SR	Soprano Recorder
AR	Alto Recorder
TR	Tenor Recorder
BR	Bass Recorder

Percussion

HD	Hand Drum
FC	Finger Cymbals
Ti	Timpani
Tr	Triangle
Tam	Tambourine

Pitched Percussion (Orff Instruments)

SG	Soprano Glockenspiel
AG	Alto Glockenspiel
SX	Soprano Xylophone
AX	Alto Xylophone
BX	Bass Xylophone
SM	Soprano Metallophone
AM	Alto Metallophone
BM	Bass Metallophone

Stringed Instruments

Gtr	Guitar
Bs	Bass
Vc	Cello
Bor	Bordun (or Cello)

Introduction

This second of three books in the **Recorder Improvisation and Technique** series is an intermediate course. Extending the lessons of **RIT One**, it develops improvisation skills, and immerses students further in music composition.

True to its title, recorder technique is also covered. By the final lessons in this book, proficiency on the instrument can be attained. More important, students can use the book as a vehicle for improvisation and invention. In fact, the engaged student will see that the lessons can apply much more broadly, to other instruments and to voice as well.

By Lesson 6, the student is improvising variations by ear. Starting with Lesson 7, the student begins a comprehensive understanding of the diatonic modes. It will be readily apparent this is not simply a "recorder method" book.

The last two lessons, on shifting-chord accompaniments and paraphony (parallel melodic movement), are an open doorway to a musical life that embraces improvisation and composition. As my mother said repeatedly, what she most admired about the Orff approach was that it introduced students to the materials of music, so that students acquired confidence and proficiency developing musical ideas - just as a composer does. Requiring a higher level of technical ability and theoretical understanding than **RIT One**, which is an introductory work, **RIT Two** makes the transition from the classroom to the real world of music.

It also prepares the way for the next and final book in the series, **RIT Three**. Picking up where this book leaves off, **RIT Three** embarks on a grand exploration and appreciation of a wonderful musical mix. Take songs of Medieval Europe, blend in a modernist respect for Indonesian and African layered subtleties of melody and rhythm, then add in North America's musical traditions, and individual improvisation. Wow. Well, let's just say there's a lot more to come.

Anne M Carley
Charlottesville, VA

Original Introduction to the Second Edition

Recorder Improvisation and Technique Book Two, like Book One, is designed to parallel and supplement the basic material in the Orff Schulwerk publications, and to spell out in detail how the sequence can best be applied to learning and teaching the recorder.

Book Two expands the materials to include hexatonic and diatonic major scales and their related modes until the whole range of the instrument to high B on the soprano and high E on the alto has been explored through exercises, improvisation, and repertoire.

New notes are introduced first with silent practice until the muscular movements are familiar; then aurally, in echo-play and phrase-building exercises. Only then are students expected to read the new note combinations.

Historical techniques - of melodic ornamentation and variation, of paraphony, and of improvising over shifting chords - are introduced at this level, and free solo improvisation is encouraged.

The first three lessons provide a review of pentatonic scales and modes, transferred to the alto recorder. When the fingering patterns are recognized, the switch to alto fingerings proves much easier than in the traditional approach - particularly when reinforced through improvisation and playing familiar tunes by ear.

Lessons 4 through 7 move into hexatonic and full major scales in F, C, G, and B♭. We then move into the diatonic modes - Aeolian, Dorian, Phrygian, and Mixolydian - in turn, with technical exercises, improvisation over the ensemble, and carefully selected repertoire from both the Western folk tradition and historical examples from the Middle Ages and the Renaissance. Students are now expected to switch freely back and forth between C and F fingerings as the repertoire and their preference determine.

The final chapter concentrates on the two historical accompanying techniques of shifting chords (I-ii and I-iii in major scales; i-VII and i-III in minor modes) and various styles of paraphony from Organum to Faux Bourdon, from parallel octaves to parallel thirds and sixths.

Isabel McNeill Carley
Brasstown, NC

PART I ~ PENTATONIC MODES

Lesson 1

Set I Pentatonic Fingerings

F Pentatonic on AR

Review of Pentatonic Modes

1. Echo what you hear

   • On your Soprano recorder in **C** Pentatonic.

   • On your Alto recorder in **F** Pentatonic.

   What relationship did you observe between the two scales?

2. Here is a chart of **Pentatonic Fingerings, Set I,** which produces **C** Pentatonic on the Soprano recorder and **F** Pentatonic on the Alto.

SR:_____

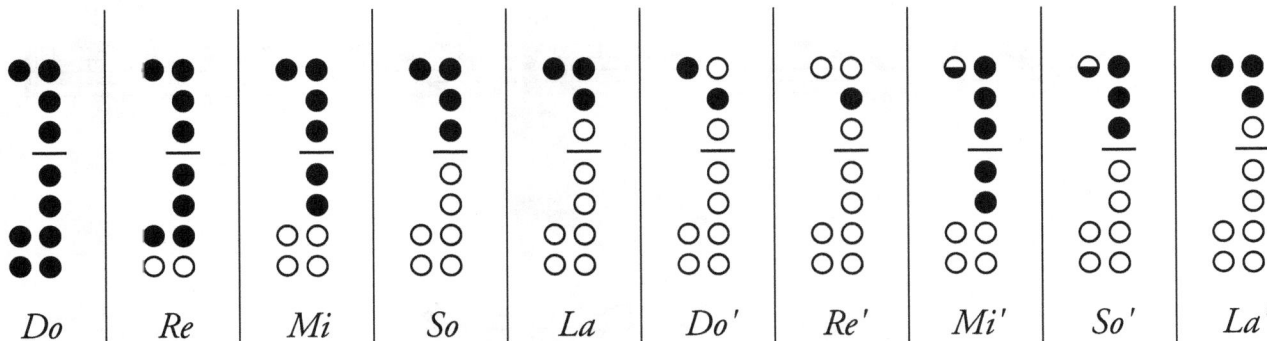

| Do | Re | Mi | So | La | Do' | Re' | Mi' | So' | La' |

AR:_____

Fill in the note names for both Soprano (SR) and Alto (AR) recorder.

For the four Sets of Fingerings, see Page 73.

3. Follow Teacher's hand signs in **F** Pentatonic on your Alto recorder. (See Page i, and **RIT One**, Page iii, for more on hand signs and the Pentatonic scales.)

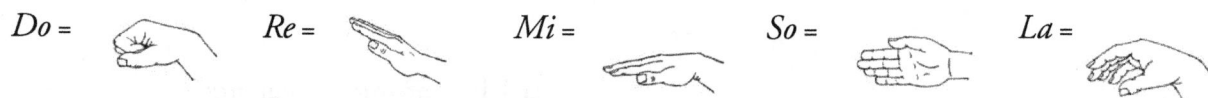

Do =   *Re* =   *Mi* =   *So* =   *La* =

4. Take turns leading the class in hand-sign improvisation on Alto recorders in **F** Pentatonic, over a supporting bordun on BX and complementary ostinato patterns on AX and SG. What notes will you now need for your bordun? _____ and _____

5. Echo Teacher's phrases in *Do* Pentatonic and *La* Pentatonic
   • On your Alto recorders
   • Singing the syllables
   • Singing the note names
   • Playing again, *thinking* the names of the notes.

   See Page 37 and **RIT One** Pages 62-63 for more on Pentatonic Modes.

6. Play what you see, observing all the articulation and dynamic markings.
   Note: Music for the Alto recorder is written at pitch, not an octave lower like music for the Soprano recorder. For example, the **F** on the top line of the treble staff, when played on AR, is the same one you're accustomed to playing on the first space of the treble staff on your SR.

7. Finger the notes with your recorder resting on your chin while you sing the note names in the three
following tunes. Play, observing all the articulation.

Down in the Meadow

North Carolina

Jig

Isabel Carley

Block Island Tune

New York

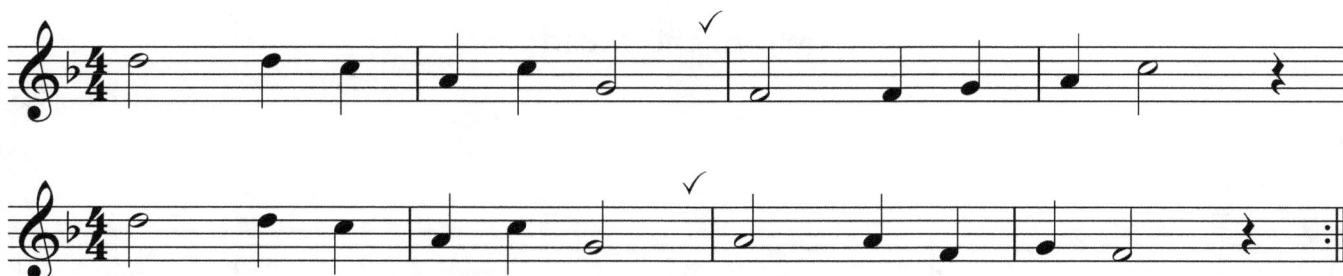

8. Play Q+A on **C' D' F' G' A'**, with the whole class answering Teacher's questions at the same time, over BX and AG in *Do* Pentatonic. Again, with volunteers answering solo.

What makes a good Question? A good Answer?

Play Q+A all around the class in *La* Pentatonic and then in *Re* Pentatonic, using appropriate accompanying bordun and ostinato.

Where should the Question end
• in *La* Pentatonic? _____   the Answer? _____
• in *Re* Pentatonic? _____   the Answer? _____

Which two notes will you use for the bordun
• in *La* Pentatonic? _____ and _____
• in *Re* Pentatonic? _____ and _____

9. Play the following melodic questions in unison for volunteers to answer in the appropriate pentatonic mode:

ⓐ *La* Pentatonic, ending on **D'**

ⓑ *Re* Pentatonic, ending on **G**

10. Build up an ensemble in *Re* Pentatonic with volunteers playing BX, AX, SX, and SG. Take as much time as necessary, adding one pattern at a time, criticizing and revising as needed so that each pattern:

    • *Is becoming to the instrument*

    • *Is complementary to ALL the other patterns, both rhythmically and melodically*

    • *Reinforces the tonal center*

        and

    • *Builds the carpet of sound without any holes at phrase breaks.*

11. Once the class is satisfied with the ensemble:

    • Sing in *Re* Pentatonic, all together, over the ensemble, listening very sensitively to be able to pick up melodic ideas from other people, singing out for a phrase or two, then relaxing into a simple ostinato in your low range, until the tonality is comfortably established.

    • Choose volunteers to play one phrase each in Q+A sets of four phrases, Q+A^1, Q+A^2, then a break before the next set of four volunteers, over the same ensemble patterns.

    • Choose new volunteers to build a supporting ensemble in a different meter, as before.

    • Then play "Pass-it-on" all around the class, either singing or playing AR, whichever is more comfortable - only one phrase for each student.

12. Play the following patterns over and over, varying the tempo, dynamics, and articulation, using

   • Tongued legato

   • Staccato

   • Slurs

   • Portato

and combinations of these four basic types of articulation.

13. Play **Old Betty Larkin** at sight. Practice if necessary.

Old Betty Larkin

Kentucky

What is the pentatonic mode? _____

Lesson 2

Set II Pentatonic Fingerings

C Pentatonic on AR

1. Echo Teacher's phrases in
   - **G** Pentatonic on your Soprano recorder.
   - **C** Pentatonic on your Alto recorder.

   What do you notice about the relationship of the fingerings?

2. Write the note names produced by the fingerings for SR and AR in the chart for **Pentatonic Fingerings Set II,** as indicated.

SR:_____

| So, | La, | Do | Re | Mi | So | La | Do | Re | Mi |

AR:_____

3. Follow Teacher's hand signs in **C** Pentatonic on your Alto recorder, in *Do, Re, So,* and *La* Pentatonic modes. (Briefly.)

4. Take turns leading the class in hand-sign phrases in whichever pentatonic mode you choose, using the notes of the **C** Pentatonic scale.

5. Echo Teacher's phrases (in one or another mode of **C** Pentatonic)
   - On your Alto recorder
   - Singing the syllables of the phrase you just played
   - Singing the note names while silently fingering your instrument
   - Playing Alto recorder again, *thinking* which notes you're playing.

6. Two or three volunteers improvise phrases for the class to echo on their Alto recorders in the same way, varying meter and mode from one leader to the next.

7. Use a phrase from the previous exercise as a melodic question for the entire class to use in Q+A play around the class.
   - Those who don't feel ready to participate may pass.
   - Teacher plays an accompanying ostinato pattern on a hand drum or BX in the appropriate pentatonic mode to support the improvisation.

8. In *La* Pentatonic, improvise a new question in **4** meter over the teacher's BX pattern. Listen to a few, and choose one to use as a melodic question.

9. Then ask for volunteers to lead the class in improvised answers with hand signs while the teacher plays a supporting ostinato on BX. The result would then be:
   - TUTTI Question - TUTTI Answer #1, led by volunteer 1
   - TUTTI Question - TUTTI Answer #2, led by volunteer 2
   - TUTTI Question - TUTTI Answer #3, led by volunteer 3
   - TUTTI Question - TUTTI Answer #4, led by volunteer 4.

   Repeat with a new Question, four new volunteers, and a new BX accompaniment.

10. Finger the following exercises silently while you say or sing the note names. Play slowly as written, using tongued legato.

    Practice:
    - Staccato
    - Slurring all seconds and playing all skips staccato.

11. Finger the next tune silently while saying the note names. Then play over Teacher's drum ostinato.

Hop Up, My Ladies

United States

Hop up, my la - dies,   three in a row,   Hop up, my la - dies, three in a row,

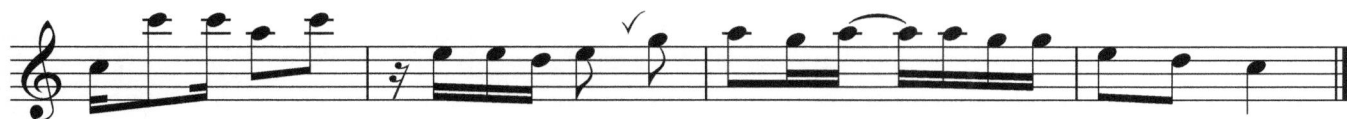

Hop up, my la - dies,   three in a row, Don't mind the wea-   ther so the wind don't blow.

HD

12. Play the following four tunes at sight. You may recall the second one from **RIT One**, Lesson 5.

Mary Mack

Georgia (United States)

ⓐ

Come Up, Horsey

Southern United States

ⓑ

Hush My Babe

Tennessee

Jack of Diamonds

North Carolina

13. In which pentatonic mode does each of the four songs in Step 12 lie?

    ⓐ _____

    ⓑ _____

    ⓒ _____

    ⓓ _____

Lesson 3

Set III Pentatonic Fingerings

B♭ Pentatonic on AR

1. Echo what you hear

   • On your Soprano recorder in **F** Pentatonic

   • On your Alto recorder in **B♭** Pentatonic.

2. The fingerings for these pentatonic scales belong to **Set III**. Write the note names for SR above the fingerings and those for AR below them in this chart.

SR: _____

| So , | La , | Do , | Re | Mi | So | La | Do' | Re' | Mi' |

AR: _____

3. Follow Teacher's hand signs, playing in **B♭** Pentatonic on your Alto recorder.

4. Take turns leading the class with hand signs in a set of four related phrases. Be ready to repeat any that the class doesn't play to your satisfaction the first time, without breaking the rhythm.

5. Echo Teacher's phrases in *La* Pentatonic on your Alto recorder.

    • Sing the names of the notes you just played, and do the hand signs

    • Sing the note names and finger silently

    • Play again, thinking the notes you're playing.

    Once the procedure is familiar, keep going without any breaks in the rhythm.

6. Play the following exercises four times each.

    Practice as needed, varying the articulation and tempo.

7. Build an ensemble in *La* Pentatonic using the **B♭** Pentatonic scale. Which two notes will you need to use in your bordun? _____ and _____

    Remember:

    • *The lowest instrument must establish the tonal center.*
    • *Other parts should use contrary motion as much as possible.*
    • *There should be rhythmic tension between the parts.*
    • *Each part should fit its own instrument.*

    Listen very critically until the carpet of sound satisfies the class.

    Then go around the class, Q+A • Q+A, in sets of four phrases, with four measures between sets.

    Three sets will probably be enough to remember.

    Which sets were most convincing? Why?

    What devices did the players use to make their conversations hang together?

8. Repeat the whole procedure with a new group of volunteers on the bar instruments, and new sets of four recorder players.

   Which sets worked better this time?

   Why?

9. Echo Teacher's phrases in *Re* Pentatonic.

10. Follow Teacher's hand signs in *Re* Pentatonic.

    Which note is the tonic? _____

    Which is the dominant? _____

    What is its hand sign? _____

    Which note is the seventh degree of the scale? _____

    What is its hand sign? _____

11. Four volunteers lead the class with hand-sign phrases, Q+A • Q+A, over Teacher's BX accompaniment, in *Do*, *La*, or *Re* Pentatonic, as the BX part requires.

12. Choose one of the Question phrases from Step 11 for the whole class to play while volunteers lead the class in hand-sign Answer phrases.

    Establish the tonality with two or three accompanying bar instruments.

    The Question phrase will determine the pentatonic mode to be used.

13. Play the following tunes, at sight. Practice as necessary to be ready to play them in class.

Chippewa Flute Melody

United States

legato

From "Sing It Yourself," Louise Larkin Bradford, Alfred Publishing Co. Inc. 1978. Used with permission.

Colorado Trail

United States

Andante

PART II ~ HEXATONIC MODES

Lesson 4

F Hexatonic

F Major

Fa and *Ti* Hand Signs

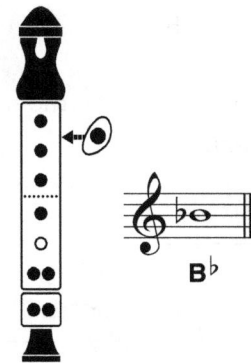

Alto Recorder　　　　　　Alto Recorder

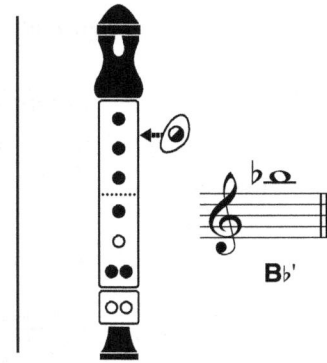

1.　Many tunes which are nominally major are actually six-tone or Hexatonic, using one or the other of the half step intervals, *Fa* and *Ti*, but not both. The awkward interval of the augmented fourth is thus completely avoided, both melodically and harmonically, until later. *Fa* and *Ti* are first introduced as passing tones, filling in the gaps in the pentatonic scale.

If **F** is *Do*, then **B♭** is *Fa* and its hand sign looks like this:

Fa =

Since **B♭** is already familiar, the only problem is the new fingering combinations. Practice going back and forth across the **B♭** between **A** and **C'**, and then farther afield, as in the following exercises.

Play them silently, concentrating on the fingering combinations.

Then play aloud, four times each.

How many different ways can you play each pattern, varying the tonguing and dynamics?

2. Echo Teacher's *Fa*-Hexatonic phrases in **F**. Use supporting bordun + ostinato patterns if you wish.

3. Follow Teacher's hand signs in sets of four **F**-Hexatonic phrases using *Fa*.
   Take turns leading the class with hand signs in sets of four phrases, being ready to repeat any phrases the class fumbles without any break in the rhythm.

4. Play the following phrases silently at sight, thinking the fingerings.
   Play aloud, observing all articulation signs.
   Practice as needed.

5. Play by heart on AR in **F**:
   - *Twinkle, Twinkle, Little Star*
   - *Hush Little Baby.*

6. Play Q+A all around the class using the following melodic questions ⓐ and ⓑ, and improvising your own answers when your turn comes:
   - Singing
   - Playing AR.

   Use only the notes of **F** Hexatonic with *Fa.*

   Build a supporting ensemble with BX bordun, AX, SX, and SG ostinato patterns.

   For ⓐ, play the Question in unison and improvise two-measure Answers, in turn.

   For ⓑ, improvise four-measure Answers.

7. Finger silently the following two **F**-Hexatonic tunes. Then play. Practice as needed.

The Flora Dance

Cornwall

First of May's the Flo - ra Day,   Can you dance the Flo - ra?

Yes I can, with a fine young man,   Yes I can, with a fine young man,

Yes I can, with a fine young man,   I can dance the Flo - ra.

The Seagull

Ireland

8. Play **The Flora Dance** on your SR as if you were playing your Alto.

What key are you actually playing in? _____

The fingering patterns are exactly the same: **Set I** fingerings in both cases, with *Fa* added to the pentatonic scale.

Play **The Seagull** on your SR, transposing down the octave.

- Which tune is authentic? (*Do - Do'*) _____
- Which tune is plagal? (*So, - So'*) _____

9. To play *Ti* hexatonic in **F** requires going back and forth across **E'** to **F'** or **D'** as in the following exercises:

The Souling Song

England

10. With both *Fa* and *Ti* under your fingers, the full **F** Major scale can be used. Play it:
    - Slowly, with tongued legato
    - Faster, slurring every two notes together
    - Faster still, staccato.

11. Echo your teacher's scale tunes, starting on either low or high **F**, like these:

12. Take turns improvising scale tunes in different meters for the class to echo.

    Notice that all scale-tones must be used and that any tone may be repeated.

13. Practice the following exercises silently, concentrating on moving your fingers exactly together, particularly from **A'** to **B♭'** and from **B♭'** to **C'** or **D'**.

    Remember that high **B♭** requires one less finger than low **B♭**, *i.e.*, no RIGHT fifth finger. (See Fingering Chart, Page 72.)

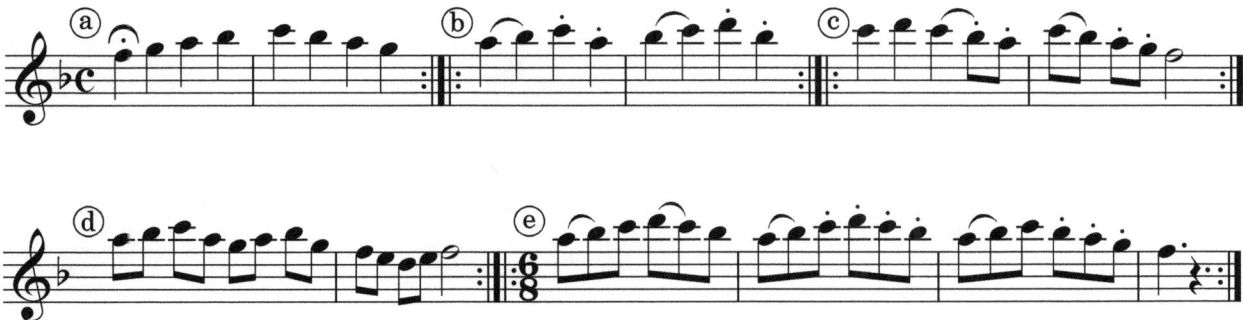

14. Follow Teacher's improvised hand-sign phrases using both *Fa* and *Ti*, which looks like this:

    Ti =

15. Take turns leading the class with hand signs in sets of four phrases, repeating any the class needs to practice as you go along. Practice with your practice partner outside of class.

16. When you are comfortable with the new notes, play **Piping Tim of Galway** with alternating choirs of Alto and Soprano recorders, as indicated.

Piping Tim of Galway

Ireland

Allegro

Lesson 5

C Hexatonic

C Major

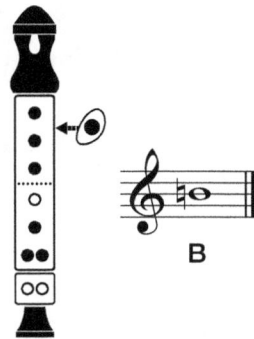

Alto Recorder   Alto Recorder

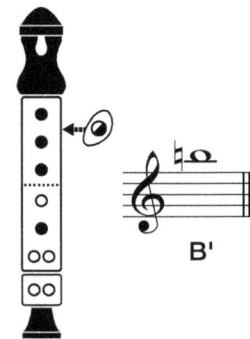

1. To play in **C** Hexatonic on AR, we need only insert *Fa* or *Ti* into the pentatonic scale, using **Set II** fingerings. For the four Sets of Fingerings, see Page 73.

Which note is now *Fa*? _____ *Ti*? _____

Echo Teacher's *Fa*-Hexatonic phrases, briefly.

Since the fingerings are already familiar from the **F** Major scale, the only problems are:

- Shifting the tonal center and becoming accustomed to the new set of syllables

- Matching hand signs for notes you already know.

Follow Teacher's hand-sign phrases, playing in **C** Hexatonic with *Fa*.

Take turns leading the class in pairs of Q+A phrases in **C** Hexatonic with hand signs.

Two or three volunteers will be enough.

Practice doing the same thing with your practice partner.

2. Play by ear:

    *   *Twinkle, Twinkle, Little Star* in **C** Hexatonic, on AR

    *   *Hush, Little Baby*, starting on low **G**, on AR in **C** Hexatonic.

3. Sing the following two American folk songs in whatever octave is most comfortable for you.
    Then finger silently while thinking the tune.

    Play **Three Little Pigs** slowly at first, and practice until you can play up to tempo.

Three Little Pigs

Virginia

Allegro

Oh, the far - mer had one, And the far - mer had two, And the far - mer had

three lit - tle pigs in a stew, Tra - la - la, La la la la la la la

la, La la la la la la la la la la la.

By'm Bye

Texas

Slow

By'm bye, By'm bye, Stars shi - ning, num - ber, num - ber one, num - ber

two, num - ber three, Good Lord, by'm bye, by'm bye, Good Lord, by'm bye.

4. Play both tunes again, in **F** Hexatonic, starting

   • **A B♭ C B♭ A G** on **Three Little Pigs** and

   • **F' C__ F' C__** on **By'm Bye**.

5. To play *Ti* Hexatonic in the key of **C** we need to play **B♮** in both octaves.

   Play the following patterns:

   • As written

   • An octave higher.

   Think which fingers have to be lifted in each new combination.

   Be very careful to move your fingers exactly together so that no extra sounds are heard between the written notes.

   When your fingers move precisely, you can actually hear the pitches without blowing at all.

   Practice as needed, varying both tonguing and tempo.

   Note: On some recorders, these standard fingerings for **B♮** may prove sharp, and you will need to cover part or all of the bottom hole to get them in tune.

   Check your own instrument carefully so that you can add the extra finger immediately if necessary.

6. Echo play around the class on **G A B C D E**, with each person improvising a new *Ti* Hexatonic phrase for the class to echo without losing the beat. It will be much easier with an underlying bordun on BX. If **C** is the tonal center, what notes will be used? _____ and _____

7. Follow Teacher's hand signs in *Ti* Hexatonic in **C** on your Alto recorder. Practice doing the same thing with your practice partner, and be ready to lead the class next time.

8. Practice the following melodic questions on AR until everyone is secure.

   Then go around the class asking the question in unison.

   Take turns making up the answers in either *Fa* or *Ti* Hexatonic, as you choose, over Teacher's drum
   ostinato or bordun.

Lesson 6

G Major
Set IV Fingerings
Variations

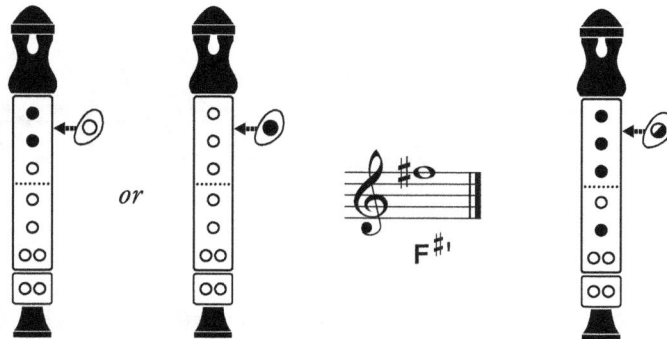

Alto Recorder   Soprano Recorder

*For Low **F♯** diagrams, see Page 27.*

1. To play the full **G**-Major scale, we need to play high **F♯**. Practice the following combinations silently on your Alto. Then play, slowly and precisely. If you are not yet ready to switch back to playing Soprano recorder, come back to it later when the Alto fingerings are secure.

2. Echo Teacher's scale tunes in **G** major. Then take turns improvising your own, for the class to echo. Go either up or down the scale, repeating any notes you choose without changing direction, like this:

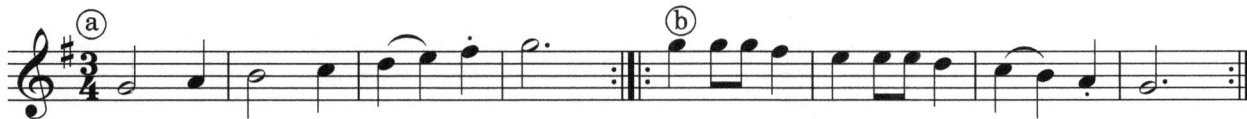

3. How many songs can you play by ear in the key of **G** on your Alto? Try *Aunt Nancy*, *Yankee Doodle*, *Skip to My Lou*, and the *Doxology*, to start with.

4. Two scale canons:

Practice ⓑ with the articulation suggested.

When that is secure, change the slurring patterns and increase the tempo.

Choose a particular tonguing pattern, and play in two- or three-part canon.

Here, for example, are some alternatives:

Now pick up your Soprano Recorder and play ⓑ again.

Which **Set** of fingerings are you now using? _____. For the four Sets of Fingerings, see Page 73.

Play ⓑ again on your SR, *as if* you're playing your AR. What scale are you actually using? _____
The fingering for the new note is the same on both instruments: **F♯** on the Alto, **C♯** on the Soprano.
The fingering for the scale of **G** on the AR is exactly the same as the fingering for the scale of **D** on SR.
This is the **Set IV** fingering pattern.

5. For both instruments to play in the key of **G**:

- The Soprano uses **Set II** fingerings

- The Alto uses **Set IV**, as in the following examples, **Cherubini's Canon** and **Injun John**.

Cherubini's Canon

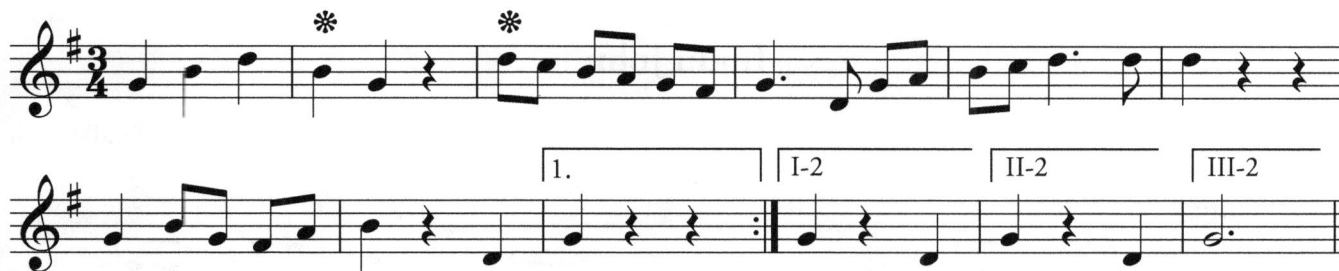

Play in unison at first, an octave higher than written, with half the class playing SR and the other half playing AR.

Reverse parts.

Then play in two-part canon, with SR leading and AR following one bar later.

How will you divide the parts for a three-part canon?

Learn to play low **F♯** on AR and SR. You'll use it in the next two pieces.

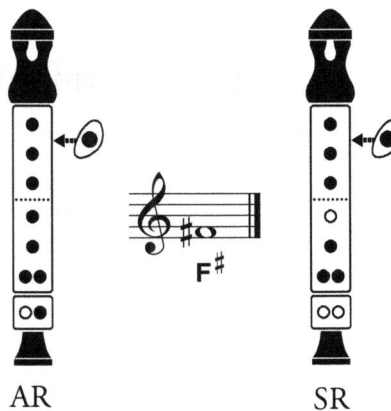

F♯

AR   SR

Injun John

American Fiddle Tune

Pay close attention to

- SR octave transposition compared to AR playing at pitch
- Articulation.

Divide AR players into two sections for the next piece.

Fiddle Tune

United States

Try this Hand Drum part:

Hot Cross Buns (Variations)

6. Play **Hot Cross Buns** in **G**, starting on high **B**, from memory. Then change it into a waltz, beginning:

7. Change it into a pompous march, beginning:

8. Change it into a skipping dance, starting like this:

9. Change it into a sprightly dance, beginning:

10. Change to the minor mode, slow and legato, starting like this:

11. Change it into a funeral march, or a tango, still in the minor mode.
Note the proportion to the original tune. *E.g.*, in Step 6, it's one bar of the waltz to one beat of the original tune; in Step 8, it's three-eighths of the skipping dance to one beat of the original, *etc.*

12. Choose another tune you know as well, and work out a similar set of variations on it to play in class. Write down the two or three you like best.

13. Go back and play both sets (Steps 6-10, and those you just wrote) on your Soprano recorder instead. You will actually be playing exactly the same notes, but with SR you are accustomed to reading them an octave lower than they sound, so you will need to transpose them down an octave as you play.

Lesson 7

B♭ Major

Pentatonic Modes

Intro to the Diatonic Modes

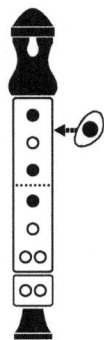

E♭
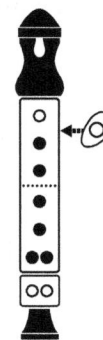

AR　　　　　　SR

1. In the key of **B♭** we need to play **E♭**.
   Practice the new finger combinations silently as Teacher calls out the note names:
   E.g., **E♭ F E♭ F** • **E♭ D E♭ D** • **D E♭ F E♭** • **E♭ G E♭ G** • **E♭ C E♭ C** *etc.*

2. Finger the following exercises silently at first. Then play, slowly and precisely, concentrating on the fingers that must be lifted together. Listen very critically to be sure that there are no extra sounds between the notes.

3. Echo what you hear Teacher play in **B♭**, using:

    *   **B♭ C D E♭ F**

    *   Full scale, **B♭** to **B♭'**

    *   Plagal scale, **F** to **F'**

    Or play, following Teacher's hand signs.

4. Play by ear:

    *   *O How Lovely Is the Evening* in **B♭**, starting on *Do*

    *   *Skip to My Lou*, starting on *Mi.*

5. With your practice partner, take turns improvising melodies over a recorder ostinato in **B♭**, like these:

6. Play Q+A all around the class over Teacher's ostinato on BX, in sets of four phrases, [A] [B] [A] [B], with an interlude between sets. Try to remember which phrases made the best questions, which made the best answers, which pairs added up best, which sets made the most musical sense. What was the relation between the Q+A phrases in the most successful combinations? Were all four phrases "talking on the same subject"?

7. Choose three or four people to go to the bar instruments to build a carpet of sound to support two or three more sets of improvised phrases in **B♭**. Take plenty of time building the ensemble so that the parts are complementary, without parallel movement, and appropriate to the chosen instruments. The lowest instruments are restricted to the tonic and its fifth; those in the middle range may use a few more tones; those in the highest range may use thirds and seconds which would muddy the ensemble in lower voices.

    Remember:

    *   *The more instruments there are in the ensemble, the less each can do.*

    *   *The fewer instruments in the ensemble, the more each can do.*

    Listen critically to the phrase relationships, and be ready to discuss them when the group improvisation is finished, as you would need to do teaching your own classes.

8. Improvise little pieces for movement in **B♭** - perhaps a march, a skipping dance, and a stamping dance or step-hop sequence - and be prepared to play one in class.

9. Play the following pieces at sight, and practice as needed.

The British Grenadiers

England

Allegretto, marcato

Dick's Maggot *

Playford, 1703

Sauntering

*At the time, "maggot" meant a whim, fancy or silly idea, and described dance tunes that were hard to categorize.

Try both previous tunes on SR using AR fingerings. What key are you now playing in? _____

10. Play the following Dance over the hand drum ostinato, and improvise your own answers to the melodic question in the **B** section:

- Singing tutti
- Playing tutti
- With volunteer soloists.

Come and Join Our Dancing

Isabel Carley

11. To play in the key of **B♭** the Soprano recorder must play both low and high **E♭**, which are fingered like this:

(The same fingering will produce **A♭** on AR.)

Go back and play as many exercises in Step 2 on SR as you can, in preparation for improvisation in **B♭**.

Practice **The British Grenadiers** (Step 9) on SR, and play a few familiar folk songs by ear before tackling the following three-part round for SR and AR.

Haste Thee, Nymph

John Milton   Samuel Arnold, 18th c.

- Play in unison, with half the class on SR, half on AR.
- Then play in two parts, with SR in the lead.
- Finally, in three parts, SR, AR, AR/TR.

INTRODUCTION TO THE DIATONIC MODES

The rest of this book will explore Diatonic scales and modes.

Just as we formed the complete major scales by filling in the missing half steps in *Do* Pentatonic, so we complete the diatonic modes of Western historical tradition by filling in the missing steps in the other pentatonic modes.

In whichever major scale we choose to use, we find that

- *Do* Pentatonic becomes the ***IONIAN MODE***

- *Re* Pentatonic becomes the ***DORIAN MODE***

- *Mi* Pentatonic becomes the ***PHRYGIAN MODE***

- *So* Pentatonic becomes the ***MIXOLYDIAN MODE,*** and

- *La* Pentatonic becomes the ***AEOLIAN MODE.***

The two missing modal scales - Lydian on *Fa* and Locrian on *Ti* - are of little practical use because of the inescapable augmented fourth in Lydian (**F-B**) and the diminished fifth in Locrian (**B-F**).

The Pentatonic Modes chart (Page 37) and Diatonic Modes chart (page 38) will clarify the relationships of the four "ecclesiastical modes" - Ionian, Dorian, Phrygian, and Aeolian - and the more recently used Mixolydian, which appears frequently in United States folk, blues, and pop music.

_____

12. On the following two Modes diagrams, complete the blank staffs with your own charts for **F** and **G**, to broaden your understanding of the modes and their role in improvisation and composition. For more on this topic, see **RIT One**, Pages 62-63.

PENTATONIC MODES
C Pentatonic

F Pentatonic

G Pentatonic

DIATONIC MODES

C Diatonic

Major Modes

Mixolydian (*Low 7th*)

Lydian (*Augmented 4th*)

Ionian (*Major scale*)

Dorian (*High 6th*)

Phrygian (*Low 2nd*)

Aeolian (*Low 6th*)

Minor Modes

F Diatonic

Major Modes

Minor Modes

G Diatonic

Major Modes

Minor Modes

PART III ~ DIATONIC MODES

Lesson 8

The Aeolian Mode

G♯ on Alto and Soprano

Transposition

1. The Aeolian Mode is another, much older name for the Natural Minor scale, the *La* scale which conforms exactly to the key signature. When, for instance, the Aeolian Mode starts on **A**, **A** is *La* in the scale of **C** Major, and we use the key signature of **C** Major, no sharps or flats. It is spelled **A B C' D' E' F' G' A'**. If there is one flat - **B**♭ - in the key signature, we're using the scale of **F** Major, and the Aeolian would be **D E F G A B**♭ **C' D'**.

   Sing this Aeolian scale with hand signs, in whichever octave is comfortable for you

| La | Ti | Do | Re | Mi | Fa | So | La' | So | Fa | Mi | Re | Do | Ti | La |

   Repeat in canon: high voices, then lows.
   Again, in three parts: highs, middles, lows.

2. Follow Teacher's (or a volunteer leader's) hand signs, singing - then playing - in **A** Aeolian, with patterns like these:
   * *La Ti Do Re Mi__ Mi Re Do Ti La*
   * *La Do Mi Do La So La__*
   * *La__ Mi__ La__ Mi__ Re__ Mi__ La__*
   * *Mi Re Do, Do Ti La, Ti So La La__*

3. Echo singing "Loo" each pattern that Teacher plays on AX. Repeat, with solfège syllables and hand signs. Then play on either SR or AR, and go right on to the next pattern.

4. Play what you see, and practice as needed, varying both tonguing and tempo.

5. Echo the following Question until you know it by heart. Then go round the class, asking the Question in unison and taking turns answering it, ending on **A**. Build a supporting Bordun-Ostinato accompaniment using BX, AM, AX, and triangle, taking pains to make the parts mutually complementary.

6. Play Q+A around the class in four-phrase sets over Teacher's supporting BX pattern, with brief interludes of the ongoing pattern between sets. Discuss, calling attention to the sets you liked best and pinpointing the reasons for your choice.
   Repeat, in reverse order, with opposite assignments and a new ostinato.

7. Improvise your own answers to these melodic questions, and write the best ones below.

8. With your practice partner, take turns improvising little pieces for movement in the Aeolian mode. Be sure to use the characteristic interval, the low sixth (**F**), so that your improvisation is clearly in the Aeolian. Without the sixth we can't be sure.

9. Play the following two Aeolian melodies, and practice them as needed, an octave higher than written. This means AR players should transpose up an octave, as you play.

For **Childgrove**, learn **G♯**.
Fingerings for AR in both octaves are illustrated here.
Use **G♯'** in **Childgrove**, since AR is transposing up an octave.

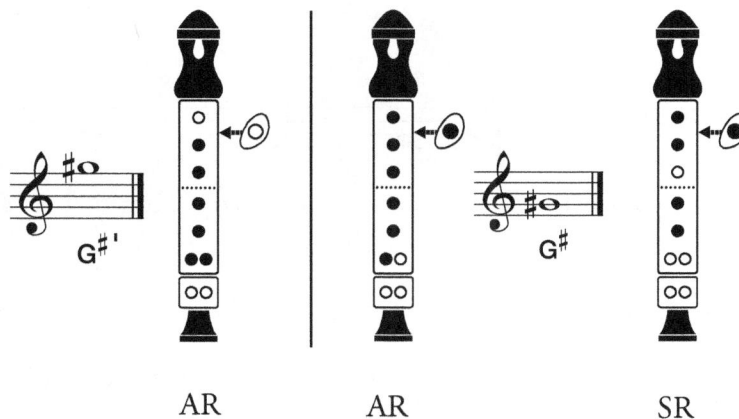

AR   AR   SR

Childgrove

English Country Dance, 17th c.

A **Allegretto**

B

Fine

Consolation

American Folk Hymn

Andante

Once more, my soul, the__ ri - sing__ day Sa - lutes thy wa-king eyes; Once__

more, my__ voice, thy tri - bute__ pay To Him that rules__ the skies.

TRANSPOSITION

The Aeolian mode may be built on any tone, not just on **A**. If you play **Consolation** on your SR using Alto fingerings, which scale will you actually be using? _____

Now that you know the major scales of **F**, **C**, **G**, and **B♭**, the corresponding Aeolian scales, built on *La*, are already under your fingers, since they require no new fingering combinations.

10. Echo Teacher's **D** Aeolian scale tunes on AR. Then take turns leading the class either up or down the scale, repeating notes as needed to bring the tune alive.

11. Play the following English folk song and practice until the unusual rhythm really flows.

Searching for Lambs

England

As   I walked out__ one May mor - ning, One May mor ning__ be - time, I
What makes you rise__ so   soon, my dear, Your jour-ney to__ pur - sue? Your

met a maid__ from home had strayed, Just as the sun__ did shine.
pret - ty feet__ they__ tread so sweet,__ Strike off the mor - ning dew.

12. Play this one an octave higher, first on your AR, then on your SR (SR does the transposing for you).

God Rest Ye Merry, Gentlemen

English Carol

13. Echo Teacher's **E** Aeolian scale tunes. Then play the scale slowly, very legato, following Teacher's hand signs.

14. Practice the following **Provençal Dance** on both AR and SR. Play in class, doubling in octaves, with half the class on SR, the other half on AR. Then take turns, as marked, ending Tutti.

Provençal Dance

Allegro

France

15. Play the scale of **G** Aeolian

    • Slowly, in unison

    • In two-part canon, SR, then AR, a third apart.

16. Build the ensemble in **G** Aeolian to support Q+A improvisation around the class in sets of four phrases. Discuss which sets proved most satisfying musically, calling attention to successful relationships between Q and A phrases.

17. Play the following two tunes, paying particular attention to achieving a real tongued legato on **Picardy**, using "d-th" tonguing on all the quarter notes; and on quick, perky playing of **Woodicock**, with a silence of articulation on all the dots, so that each sixteenth note belongs with its following eighth every time.

Picardy

France, 16th c.

Woodicock

England, 17th c.

Lesson 9   The Dorian Mode

1. The Dorian mode is the diatonic scale on *Re*, a minor scale with a high sixth - **B**♭ in its **D** position. It was widely used throughout the Western world, both in ecclesiastical and secular music through the Sixteenth Century, and has survived in unaccompanied folk songs until our own day.

   Sing the Dorian scale with hand signs until it's in your ears. Then play it on your Alto recorder, slowly, as legato as possible, before doing it in canon - in two parts, then in three parts - listening very critically to the intonation so that all the intervals and triads are in tune.

   Re   Mi   Fa   So   La   Ti   Do   Re'   Do   Ti   La   So   Fa   Mi   Re

2. Echo Teacher's phrases in the Dorian mode.
   Note: Unless the characteristic interval, the high sixth, occurs in the tune, it is impossible to tell whether it is Dorian or Aeolian or some other minor scale.

3. Practice the following exercises at different tempi, different dynamic levels, and with as many different tonguing patterns as you can devise:

4. Play the following scale exercise in canon

   • In class, on both SR and AR

   • With your practice partner.

5. Play Q+A around the class in the Dorian mode over a **D-A** bordun pattern on BX and an AG ostinato, in sets of four phrases with an interlude between phrases.

   Listen very critically for the most successful pairs and sets, and be prepared to be specific in your observations, as you would need to be in your own classrooms.

   For example:

OSTINATO PATTERNS:

Repeat

   • With new accompanying patterns in a different meter, and

   • With volunteers leading the class with hand signs in a Dorian improvisation.

Take your time in building the ensemble, so that

   • The holes in the BX part are filled by the higher instrument(s)

   • There is rhythmic tension between the parts, and

   • Each pattern is becoming to the instrument that plays it.

6. Practice improvising your own Q+A phrases in Dorian, repeating your question with a new answer, so the form is [A] [B] [A] [C].

   Where will the questions usually end? How can you make the answers musically convincing?

7. Play Q+A again, in groups of three, with the first player in each trio playing the same question again, after number two has played an answer.

   Volunteers play supporting accompanying patterns on bar instruments, starting first and continuing between the sets.

   Reassign roles, so that everyone who wishes has a turn asking the questions.

   Which sets were most effective? Why?

8. Here is a selection of four songs in the Dorian mode, two from the Medieval period and two folk songs, one from France, and the other from the Southern Appalachians.

Como Poden

Cantigas de Santa Maria, 13th c.

Optional Drum part:

Basse Danse "Jouissance Vous Donnerai"

France, 15th c.

Noël Nouvelet

France, 17th c.

The Outlandish Knight

Southern Appalachians

He fol-lowed her up, he fol-lowed her down, And in - to the room where she

lay; She_ had not the power to flee from his arms, Nor the tongue to say_ him nay.

9. Work out the following Rondo in class, playing the [A] section tutti. Assign small groups of soloists the [B] and [C] sections. Choose four volunteers to play the new [D] section using Q+A phrases over a carpet of sound in the Dorian mode.

Dorian Rondo

Isabel Carley

Allegretto

[music notation]

[D] Q+A Improvisation over Bordun-Ostinato accompaniment.

Practice improvising new sections in the Dorian mode with your practice partner, with one playing the accompaniment and the other playing the recorder or singing. Take turns, using different accompanying instruments in different meters and moods. Here are some examples:

PATTERNS:

AM: **AM:**   **AX/BX:**

[music notation: examples labeled ⓐ, ⓑ, ⓒ]

Lesson 10   The Phrygian Mode

1. The Phrygian Mode corresponds to the white notes of the piano from **E** to **E'**. The characteristic interval is the minor second from **E** to **F**.

    Although it held an important place in European liturgical music for hundreds of years, it has almost completely vanished from the folk tradition.

    Because of their intense dislike of the interval of the diminished fifth, *diabolus in musica* (Latin for "devil in music"), early European theorists avoided the use of **B** as the dominant, changing it to **C** in the authentic position and to **A** in the plagal position.

    This emphasis works very well in unaccompanied melody or with simple tonic drones.

    We will use the fifth as the dominant and the usual **I-V** bordun, for the most part.

    Take time to get familiar with the scale:

    *   Sing the Phrygian scale with syllables and hand-signs until it's in your ears

    *   Then play, slowly and legato in unison, an octave higher than written, on either SR or AR

    *   Finally, play in three-part canon, TR at pitch, if possible, AR, then SR, listening very critically that the triads are all in tune.

Mi Fa So La Ti Do Re Mi   Mi Re Do Ti La So Fa Mi

2. Echo Teacher's scale patterns from **E** to **E'**, in either direction, like these:

3. Take turns improvising similar scale patterns all around the class:

   • Playing for the class to echo, or

   • Leading the class with hand-signs, as you choose.

4. Play Pass-it-on all around the class in the Phrygian mode, contributing one phrase each, without losing the rhythmic continuity established by Teacher's BX ostinato.

   Play either SR or AR, as you choose.

   Here are a few patterns for you to try:

5. Answer Teacher's (or a volunteer's) melodic questions in the Phrygian mode

   • First, tutti

   • Then, one by one, over the ensemble.

   Practice Q+A in Phrygian mode, both with your practice partner and by yourself, asking and answering your own questions.

   Can you repeat your questions after playing your answer?

   Can you repeat your whole Q+A^1 | Q+A^2 tune?

Phrygian Rondo (Improvised)

6. Use one of the four-phrase Q+A sets from the class as the **A** section of a Phrygian Rondo, with solo improvisations by volunteers for the contrasting **B** and **C** sections, over the ensemble. Choose a different set of players and instruments to accompany each section:

   • Perhaps BX and AG for **A**

   • AM and SG + finger cymbals for **B**

   • Timpani on **E**, AX and SX + Maracas for **C**.

   Take your time working out the accompaniments so that each part is heard and really contributes to the whole effect.

7. Improvise your own answers to the following melodic questions and write the best ones below:

8. Practice improvising Phrygian tunes over ostinati such as these, sometimes using a set form, sometimes freely, as your musical ideas require.

9. Work out ostinati to support this melody and write the best in the space below:

Phrygian Dance

Isabel Carley

Lesson 11   The Mixolydian Mode

1. The Mixolydian Mode is a major scale built on *So*.

   The characteristic interval is the low seventh - **F♮** in the example below.

   It has been widely used both historically and in American folk, pop, and blues music.

   Sing the Mixolydian scale with syllables and hand signs in whichever octave is comfortable for your voice.

| So | La | Ti | Do | Re | Mi | Fa | So | Fa | Mi | Re | Do | Ti | La | So |

2. Echo Teacher's scale tunes in Mixolydian mode.

   Then take turns improvising similar scale tunes for the class to echo.

   Practice with your practice partner outside of class.

3. Practice the following scale patterns
   * At different tempi
   * At different dynamic levels
   * With as great a variety of tonguing patterns as you can invent.

4. Follow Teacher's hand-sign phrases in Mixolydian
   - Singing
   - Playing AR or SR.

5. Using a Question phrase from Step 4, play it all together for tutti, then solo, improvised answers all around the class over a drum or BX ostinato.

6. Over a carefully worked-out ensemble of three or four bar instruments, take turns leading the class in Q+A¹ | Q-A² four-phrase improvisations, with three people leading each section with hand signs.

   The first player in each set will show the same question twice.

   In this style of group improvisation, everyone plays together.

   Stop between sets to discuss what happened:
   - What did you like about it?
   - What relationships did you notice between the question and the two answers?
   - What constructive suggestions do you have?

Mixolydian Rondo (Improvised)

7. Improvise a **Mixolydian Rondo.**
   - Use one of the four-phrase melodies from Step 6 as the [A] section of a Mixolydian Rondo
   - A small group works out accompanying patterns for each section on the bar instruments
   - Volunteers improvise the [B] and [C] episodes, or
   - Volunteers lead the whole group in hand-sign improvisation.

Or, if you prefer, use this **Mixolydian Rondo** as your Rondo Theme and **B** section.

Mixolydian Rondo

Isabel Carley

PATTERNS:

8. Learn the melody to **Hungarian Dance** by heart, and practice it on whatever recorders you have - SR, AR, TR, Sopranino - so you can double it in octaves and play one register off against another as the dance is repeated.

Hungarian Dance

Jacob Paix, 16th c.

Try playing the **Hungarian Dance** like this:

First time: **A**:   SR • AR on repeat.

                 B: SR, Bar 1 • AR, Bar 2 • both, Bar 3. Same on the repeats.

Second time: **A**:   SR + Sopranino; AR + TR on repeat.

                 B: SR + Nino on Bar 1 • AR + TR on Bar 2 • Tutti on Bar 3. Repeat.

Third time: **A**:   AR + TR • add SR and Nino on repeat.

                 B: Lows, Bar 1 • Highs, Bar 2 • Tutti on Bar 3.

9. Here are two of the many American folk songs in Mixolydian.

Old Joe Clarke

Tennessee

Whoopee-Ti-Yi-Yo

Texas

1. As I was a-walk-ing one mor-ning for plea-sure, I
2. His hat was thrown back, and his spurs was a jing-lin', And

spied a cow-pun-cher a-lo-pin' a-long. Whoo-pee
as I ap-proached he was sing-in' this song:

ti - yi - yo, Git a - long, lit-tle do-gies, For you know that Wy-o-ming-'ll

be your new home, Whoo-pee ti - yi - yo, Git a - long, lit-tle do-gies, For you

know that Wy - o - ming - 'll be your new home.

10. Once **Old Joe Clarke** and **Whoopee-Ti-Yi-Yo** are thoroughly familiar, transpose them to other Mixolydian scales by ear on both SR and AR.

11. Make your own collection of American folk songs in the Mixolydian mode. There are a great many, particularly from the South, both spirituals and blues.

PART IV ~ SHIFTING CHORDS & PARAPHONY

Lesson 12

Shifting Chords

1. Many diatonic tunes, both major and modal, are far older than the functional, cadential harmony of the last three hundred years, and are better accompanied by shifting chord patterns.

   The famous English summer canon *Sumer is icumen in* is the earliest example of this technique. (See Murray, **Orff-Schulwerk Music for Children** Volume II, p. 80.)

   In a major scale, the chord shifts are usually **I-ii**, as in the *Sumer* canon, or **I-vi**.

   The corresponding shifts in minor scales are **i-VII** and **i-III**.

   Which chord shifts are implied in the following melodies?

   Play **Goddesses** on SR and AR.

Goddesses

Playford, 17th c.

Mode? _____

What are the implied chords in Ⓐ? _____

Play **Lord Carnarvan's Jig** on SR and AR.

Lord Carnarvan's Jig

Playford, 17th c.

What is the Mode? _____

Play **The Old Mole** on AR.

The Old Mole

Playford, 17th c.

CHORD PATTERN:

2. Write the chord names and/or chord numerals under the tunes above.

   Which chord shift is used in **Goddesses?** _____

   Which in **Lord Carnarvan's Jig?** _____

   Which in **The Old Mole?** _____

The Drunken Sailor

American Sea Shanty

Solo: What shall we do with the drun-ken sai-lor? What shall we do with the drun-ken sai-lor?
Chorus: Way_____ hay__ and up she ri - ses, Way_____ hay__ and up she ri - ses,

What shall we do with the drun-ken sai-lor? Ear - lye in the mor - ning.
Way_____ hay__ and up she ri - ses, Ear - lye in the mor - ning.

AX /
BX

3. Improvise a broken-chord melody over the **i-VII** chord pattern from **The Drunken Sailor.**

   • Singing in your own comfortable range

   • Later, playing whichever recorder is easier to improvise on.

For example:

d   d   d   C   C   C

4. Using the same chord pattern, add passing tones to your tune, like this:

d   d   d   C   C   C

Continue

5. Over the same chord pattern
   - Improvise answers
   - Singing and playing to the melodic questions below, and
   - Write down your best ones.

Q: **A:**

d   d   d   C   C

Q:

C   d   d   d

A1:   **A2:**

C   C   d   C   C   d

6. Improvise a whole new tune over the same chord pattern, changing the tempo, meter, and instrumentation. Change chord positions, use "oom-pah" patterns of broken chords, or bass drones on chord roots, as you choose.

7. In groups of three, take turns improvising Q+A^1 | Q+A^2 sets on your recorders over chordal patterns such as these:

Which modes could you use for pattern ⓐ? _____

For ⓑ? _____

8. In major keys, the other most frequently used chord shift pattern is from **I** to **vi**, as in the following example:

9. Practice improvising on your recorder over the same chord progression in the keys of **C** Major, **G** Major, and **F** Major. Take turns at the accompanying bar instruments, working out complementary parts to support the melody. Begin with broken chords in your tune, and then fill in the holes with passing tones. Use one or two rhythmic motives to provide both unity and vitality.

10. In the minor modes - Aeolian, Dorian and Phrygian - the equivalent chord shift is from minor tonic, **i**, to major mediant, **III**, as in this song:

Sh-Ta-Da-Ra-Day

Irish American

Rocking gently

Sh - ta - da - ra - day,   sh - ta - day,   Times   is   migh - ty   hard_____   A

dol - lar   a   day   is   all   they   pay   for   work   on   the   bou - le - vard.

11. Practice improvising over the following chord patterns in the same way.

- In ⓐ, in whichever minor mode you choose

- In ⓑ, in Aeolian mode

Lesson 13

Paraphony

Organum

Faux Bourdon

1. Once we start using hexatonic or diatonic scales, it becomes possible to double the melody

    •   At the octave

    •   The fifth

    •   The fourth

    •   The third, or

    •   The sixth.

    Europeans discovered this in the Middle Ages. To double a melody means to add parallel parts that follow the rhythms and intervals of the original melody. This is called "Paraphony," and is pronounced "Par-APH-ony."

    "Organum," pronounced "OR-gan-um," is a style of Paraphony that uses octaves, fifths, fourths, and combinations of these intervals.

    There are numerous examples, such as this, from Ninth-Century Europe:

Sit Gloria

By the Twelfth Century, Paraphony with parallel thirds was widely used, as in this **Hymn to St. Magnus.**

Hymn to St. Magnus

Worcester Ms., 12th c.

No- bi - lis,   hu - mi - lis,   Mag- ne, mar-tyr   sta - bi - lis,   sta - bi - lis___

Parallel triads were also introduced, both in root position and in first inversion. (In first inversion, the root of the triad moves up an octave, so the third is on the bottom, the fifth is in the middle and the root is on top.)

First-inversion parallel triads, originally developed in England, became known as *Faux Bourdon* when imported into France.

The following is a lovely example from late Thirteenth-Century England.

Beata Viscera

Britain, late 13th c.

2. Practice the following scale melodies in class, listening very critically to your intonation, so that all the triads sound in tune. Notice that the interval of the diminished fifth is always avoided by sharping the fifth. See Lesson 10 for more on this interval, called "*diabolus in musica*" by Medieval theorists.

3. Note: All these historical Paraphony techniques work best in arranging stepwise melodies.

   Practice the American folk song, **Bobby**, doubling
   - A third above the melody
   - A sixth below
   - A fifth above
   - A fourth below.

   In this tune, be sure to avoid the diminished fifth, by sharping the **F** when playing a fifth above, or a fourth below, every time there's a **B** in the melody.

Bobby

United States

Bob-by in the barn-yard, Bob-by in the sta-ble, Bob-by get your hair cut, Soon as you are a-ble.

4. Sometimes the melody is doubled with complete triads in either root position, as in example ⓐ, or parallel first inversions, as in ⓑ.

   Usually the parallel triads, as in ⓐ, appear an octave above the sung melody.

   Try playing the chords in ⓐ on soprano recorders with a few players on each part while the rest of the class sings. (Remember that the SR sounds an octave higher than written.)

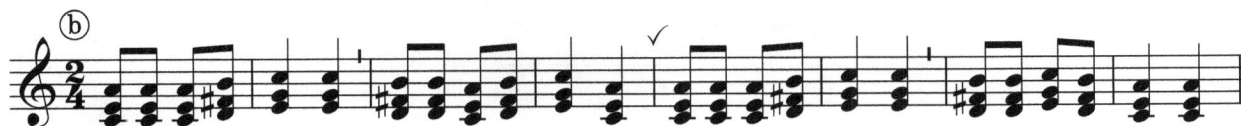

5. Work out a set of variations on **Bobby**, changing mode, meter, tempo, and timbre, with voice, SR, AR, TR, accompanying bar instruments and unpitched percussion. Use several of these paraphonic techniques.

6. Choose a mode and assign starting tones for each of two groups - either fifths, fourths, thirds, or sixths. Follow Teacher's hand-sign scalewise melodies for the lower voice while the upper voice doubles the tune at the chosen interval. Repeat, reversing assignments, so that the lower voice does the doubling. Take turns leading the class with hand signs, choosing both mode and interval.

7. Assign starting tones in triads or inversions, as in Steps 2 or 4, and improvise stepwise hand-sign melodies for one of the parts to follow while the other parts move along parallel to the part you show. Do a couple of scale echo tunes to establish the mode, before you begin.

8. Find as many modal (including Ionian) melodies that would lend themselves to paraphonic setting as you can, and choose one to work out in Faux Bourdon.

9. Arrange the Old French tune **Picardy** (introduced in Lesson 8), using as many of these historical paraphonic techniques as you can, with both voices and instruments. Add a bass drone to enrich the texture and extend the range, if you wish. You may want to transpose the tune to either **D** or **E** Aeolian for the sake of the singers.

Picardy

France, 16th c.

More to Learn

RIT Three is for the advanced student who already plays both **C** and **F** recorders.

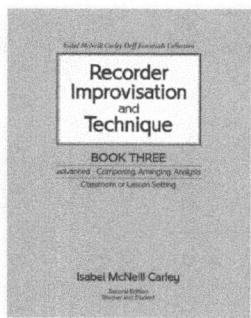

The third volume, although specific to recorder, is equally applicable to the musical development of any vocalist or instrumentalist...Carley deftly guides the player through scales, melodic ornamentation, decoration of the third, canons, chord changes, descant creation and free improvisation. She includes many fine musical examples, but the focus is the emphasis on improvisation leading to composition in the forms that parallel the history of Western music. ~ Leslie Timmons, American Recorder

Recorder Improvisation and Technique Book Three shifts the emphasis away from basic recorder instruction. These lessons focus in detail on how the Orff-Schulwerk Volumes basic sequence can be applied successfully to recorder teaching and playing. The improvisational and compositional techniques in **RIT Three** are then readily transferable to other instruments and the voice.

Compositional forms are explored with improvised materials using major, modal, and minor scales, as well as dominant and subdominant bass lines and improvised melodies. Historical, traditional, and contemporary approaches to harmony are considered, combined with improvisations using Organum, Faux Bourdon, heterophony, shifting chords, descants, and more. A final chapter explores improvisation for movement, free solo improvisation, and group improvisation.

About the RIT Book Series

A wonderful series of resource books for teaching recorder in the Orff classroom...Accessible to both experienced and inexperienced teachers...[Carley] is a master teacher. ~ Kim Kendrick, Ostinato

A wealth of practical pedagogy for learning and teaching recorder – a reflection of [Carley's] incomparable musicianship and extensive work with children and adults in ensemble settings...Especially useful for the classroom, but equally appropriate for private instruction, they provide the framework for a curriculum designed to develop comprehensive musicianship. ~ Leslie Timmons, American Recorder

To order, contact your bookseller or visit brasstownpress.com

Fingerings for Recorders in F and C

Recorder Fingering Sets I - IV

These sets apply to both **C** and **F** recorders, and may be helpful as patterns for improvisation. See the indicated Lessons for more details and context.

Set I (Lesson 1)

| Do | Re | Mi | So | La | Do' | Re' | Mi' | So' | La' |

Set II (Lesson 2)

| So, | La, | Do | Re | Mi | So | La | Do | Re | Mi |

Set III (Lesson 3)

| So, | La, | Do, | Re | Mi | So | La | Do' | Re' | Mi' |

Set IV (Lesson 6)

| Do, | Re, | Mi, | So | La | Do | Re | Mi' | So' | La' |

Brasstown Press Editions

Isabel McNeill Carley Orff Essentials Collection

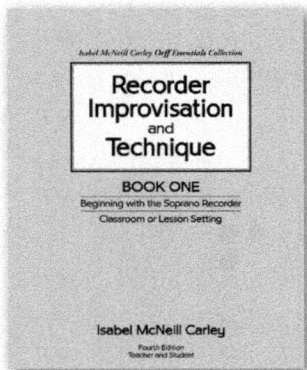

Isabel McNeill Carley Orff Essentials Collection

Recorder Improvisation and Technique

BOOK ONE

Beginning with the Soprano Recorder
Classroom or Lesson Setting

Isabel McNeill Carley

Fourth Edition
Teacher and Student

Isabel McNeill Carley Orff Essentials Collection

Recorder Improvisation and Technique

BOOK TWO

Intermediate for Alto and Soprano Recorder
Classroom or Lesson Setting

Isabel McNeill Carley

Third Edition
Teacher and Student

Isabel McNeill Carley Orff Essentials Collection

Recorder Improvisation and Technique

BOOK THREE

Advanced - Composing, Arranging, Analysis
Classroom or Lesson Setting

Isabel McNeill Carley

Second Edition
Teacher and Student

Isabel McNeill Carley Orff Essentials Collection

Making It Up As You Go

SELECTED ESSAYS

Writing About Music
Improvisation and Teaching

Isabel McNeill Carley

Eleven lessons for beginners and their teachers that explore C, G, and F Pentatonic and related modes on the soprano recorder. 46 songs and introductory exercises.
wire-o ISBN 978-1-931922-46-3
paperback ISBN 978-0-9836545-0-6

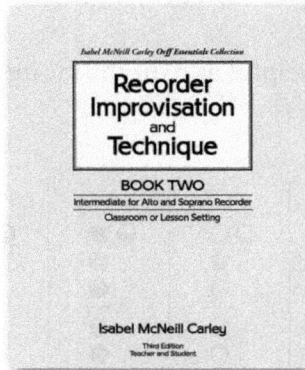

Building on RIT One, RIT Two transfers soprano fingering patterns to the alto recorder and introduces hexatonic and diatonic major and minor modes. 52 songs and intermediate exercises.
wire-o ISBN 978-1-931922-07-4
paperback ISBN 978-0-9836545-1-3

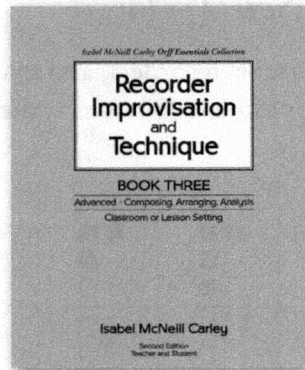

For the student already proficient on both C and F recorders. These lessons parallel the material in the Orff Schulwerk (volumes III and V). 46 challenging songs for advanced students.
wire-o ISBN 978-1-931922-08-1
paperback ISBN 978-0-9836545-2-0

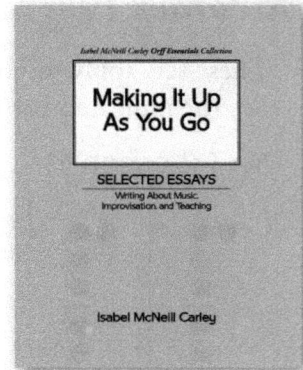

IM Carley's written work from over thirty years. The essays are grouped in three sections: Origins, Practicum, and Exhortations. Includes biographical sketch and list of IMC's publications.
ISBN 978-0-9836545-3-7

IMC's Five Little Books

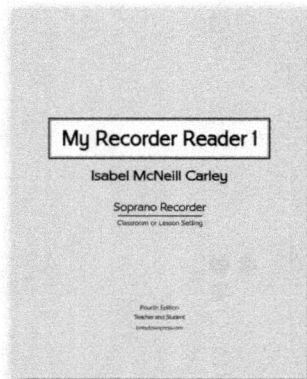

My Recorder Reader 1

Isabel McNeill Carley

Soprano Recorder
Classroom or Lesson Setting

Fourth Edition
Teacher and Student
brasstownpress.com

My Recorder Reader 2

Isabel McNeill Carley

Soprano Recorder
Classroom or Lesson Setting

Third Edition
Teacher and Student
brasstownpress.com

My Recorder Reader 3

Isabel McNeill Carley

Soprano Recorder
Classroom or Lesson Setting

Second Edition
Teacher and Student
brasstownpress.com

The three **My Recorder Reader** books are a coordinated series of songs to bring a student from elementary playing to a more experienced level. Notes are added one by one to extend the student's range, with minimal instructional comments. The carefully graduated sequence of the pieces facilitates individual mastery and skill development.

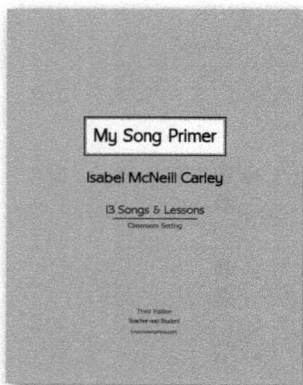

41 Songs in G Pentatonic Scale and Modes.
ISBN 978-0-9836545-6-8

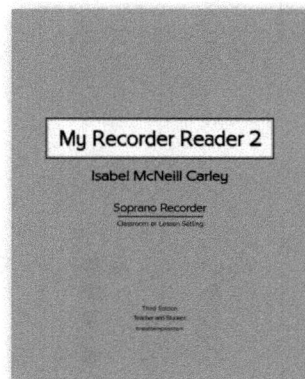

47 Songs in C Pentatonic and F Pentatonic.
ISBN 978-0-9836545-7-5

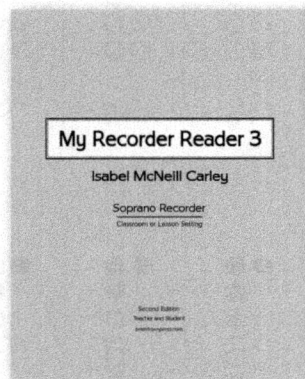

44 Songs. Expanded ranges, Pentatonic to Diatonic.
ISBN 978-0-9836545-8-2

EBOOK!

My Song Primer

Isabel McNeill Carley

13 Songs & Lessons
Classroom Setting

Third Edition
Teacher and Student
brasstownpress.com

My Recorder Primer

Isabel McNeill Carley

Soprano Recorder
Classroom Setting

Third Edition
Teacher and Student
brasstownpress.com

Establish a secure musical foundation with the step-by-step lessons offered in **My Song Primer** (for singing) and **My Recorder Primer** (for soprano recorder). Songs are interwoven in lessons with speech and rhythm exercises, suggestions for percussion and Orff instruments, and ideas for games and movement.

Taking the Orff Approach to Heart

Essays & Articles
From a Pioneer of Orff in America

Isabel McNeill Carley

First Edition
brasstownpress.com

13 Songs, one per lesson, from So-Mi to Pentatonic.
ISBN 978-0-9836545-4-4

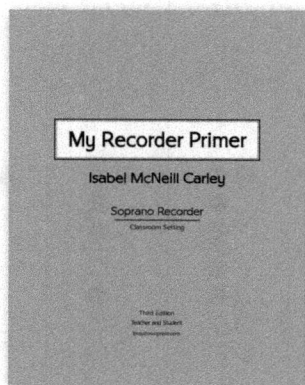

35 Songs in 6 Lessons, D-E-G-A range.
ISBN 978-0-9836545-5-1

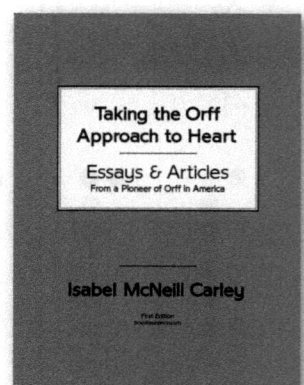

All new essays and articles plus a read-aloud story.
ISBN 978-0-9836545-9-9

Brasstown Press ✺ brasstownpress@gmail.com ✺ brasstownpress.com